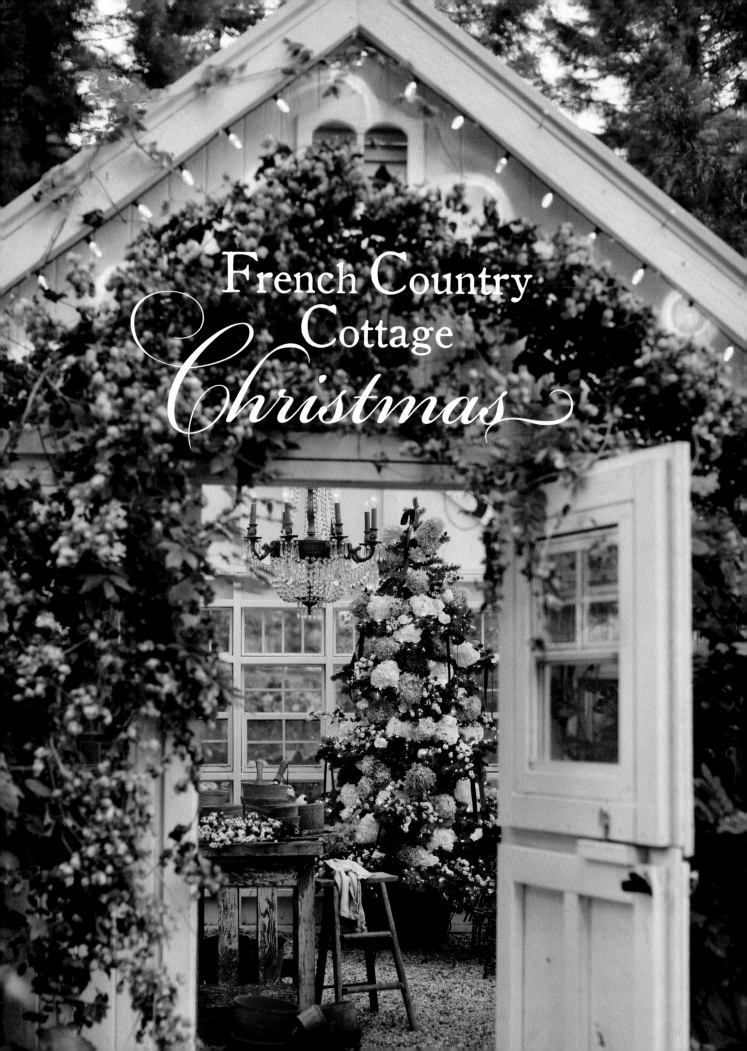

French Country Cottage
Christmas

French Country Cottage

Cottage

Christmas

Courtney Allison

Gibbs Smith

For my family—my husband, children, and grandchildren. You inspire me every day to create a home filled with the beauty and magic of Christmas all year long.

Contents

*F*ull of all things merry and bright, the Christmas
season feels magical and full of excitement. When the
trees start to twinkle for the first time each year, I am
touched with a nostalgia that takes me right back to the wonder of my
childhood. During the holidays, our house was aglow with Christmas
cheer. Every morning and night when it was dark outside, the rooms
were filled with a warm glow from the tree and fires crackling in the
fireplaces. Anticipation of the holiday season filled every room in our
home—from the decorating and baking my mom would do before the
big Santa party, to lying under the tree looking at the lights, to staring
out the breakfast nook window with my brothers and sister watching for
our grandparents to arrive on Christmas morning. Even as an adult, the
first time the tree twinkles and the Christmas music plays each season, I
feel a bit of a misty-eyed child again.

When our children were born, watching their wonder and excitement,
my husband and I experienced all that childhood enchantment through
their eyes. Setting out the cookies and milk for Santa—and the carrots
for Rudolph, of course—baking cookies, buying gifts for the community
Giving Tree, and the fun evening we would spend driving around to look
at all the houses lit up with Christmas displays were some of my favorite
things. And now, with our grandchildren, the holidays are overflowing

with childhood wonder once again. Enjoying holiday moments and memories with our family in a home full of Christmas cheer is truly the most beautiful gift of all.

When I was dating the man who would become my husband, I was nineteen and living in Montana in a second-floor studio apartment in a building full of old character and charm. I loved all its quirks, like the step up to the bathroom and the living room, which became the bedroom when the Murphy bed was pulled down. As the holiday season approached, I knew what the tree would look like that year: a simple, spindly, wispy, tree with dainty branches that would be perfect for holding just a few pretty, little baubles.

Of course, my husband was a complete opposite. His ideal Christmas tree was the chubbiest, fullest, and tallest he could manage to squeeze into his house. When we went to get our trees together, we both fully embraced our individual styles. I went home with my wee tree—sparse, and so small that the top of the tree wasn't strong enough to place a star on. But a few strands of simple white lights made it twinkle perfectly.

When I went to his house for dinner, he could hardly wait to show me his decorated fluffy tree. In contrast to mine, his was stuffed into the corner by the fireplace and filled a quarter of the room. It was covered in colorful lights and draped with what looked to be a hundred boxes of silver tinsel. When I saw his excitement, I couldn't help but smile. Just like me, with my Charlie Brown–style tree that I loved, he had found Christmas magic in the big tree that shimmered each time he walked by.

While we now appreciate both of our tree-decorating tastes, we do go-round about colorful or clear lights on occasion, though having lights that change color and allows for both options handles that. Another thing that helps to mesh our different styles is having several trees inside the house and outside, making room to fully embrace and enjoy several different looks and styles each season.

Planning Ahead

After Christmas

✳ Shop discounted decor and gifts.
✳ Shop for vintage items at thrift stores before they pack them away.

End of December & Early January

✳ Pack up, label, and store Christmas decor.
✳ Take stock of what you have, anything you don't use, and things you want to add for next year.

Summer

✳ Watch yard sales for vintage ornaments.
✳ Shop for items like jelly jars that can be used for making gifts.
✳ Pre-wrap gifts you've bought and those that will be mailed internationally.
✳ Why not plan a Christmas in July gathering for extended family to take the stress off December?
✳ Plan color schemes and ideas for your holiday decor.
✳ Order specialty items like vintage ornaments, tinsel, beaded garlands, and more.
✳ Plant the garden with herbs, flowers for drying, etc., for gifting.
✳ Order decor in shop-early specials.
✳ Order artificial trees and garlands before the rush.
✳ Spruce up indoors for holiday guests, e.g., update paint, refresh bedding, and order robes, slippers, and soft towels.

The Countdown Begins

September

- Place orders for holiday decor items.
- Harvest herbs and flowers from the garden for drying as package toppers, potpourris, etc.
- Order gifts that require personalization— monogramming, dating, etc.
- Book holiday travel early.

October

- Plant narcissus bulbs to force; pick up bulbs like amaryllis and paperwhites for forcing after Thanksgiving.
- Dry orange slices and make pomander balls.
- Order fresh garlands and wreaths to be delivered when you want them.
- Get family portraits taken.
- Start your holiday cards and finish before Thanksgiving.
- Purchase holiday stamps from the post office.
- Decide what charitable causes you will support this year and connect with local organizations.
- Mail overseas packages.

November

- Put up artificial trees before Thanksgiving if that is your tradition.
- Plan your tablescapes and food for the holidays.
- Order any fresh foods for Thanksgiving and Christmas to arrive as needed.
- Shop vintage Christmas at thrift stores.
- Order custom fresh wreaths and garlands mid-month for delivery in early December.
- Plan your cookie exchange or holiday party and send out save-the-dates.
- Start neighbor gifting around Thanksgiving to relieve pressure in December.

December

- Mail holiday cards the first week.
- Wrap gifts early for displaying under the tree.
- Mail gifts early to allow for delays in transit.
- Get the guest room linens washed and ready for visitors.
- Decorate gingerbread houses.
- Bake cookies to enjoy and gift to neighbors.
- Plan a shopping day and coffee date with close friends.
- Plan a day to relax before the big day.
- Be mindful, be present, focus on the people, smile, enjoy.

Making It Personal

❊ Scout around for an interesting vessel to hold the tree, and tinker with materials such as gravel, kitty litter, or sand to hold the stump steady.

❊ Trim a tree with ornaments handed down over the years. Heirloom is a beautiful look.

❊ Decorate a child's room with them, using their favorite color or a theme that reflects what they are crazy about at the moment.

❊ Bake or make scented shortbread or gingerbread cutout cookies, cranberry garlands, dried orange pomanders or slices (see p. 184). Add ribbons to old metal cookie cutters for whimsical ornaments.

❊ Add Christmas moments through the house—bottlebrush trees in the china cabinet, a wreath in the hallway, a crate full of ornaments and fairy lights, greenery atop a mirror, a small sprig of cedar pine tied with a ribbon on a door knob, etc.

25 Inspiring Trees

Christmas trees and their decorations are purely and ultimately a matter of personal choice, from choosing a fresh or faux tree to the color palette and types and colors of lights. Some trees are covered in oodles of ornaments, picks, and ribbons galore, while others glimmer softly with just lights and candles and a sprinkling of tinsel. Some are traditional in color and decor; others are uniquely one's own, filled with nostalgic ornaments that have been handed down or collected over many years or dressed in favorite characters, colors, or toys that reflect the family's interests. And still others are carefully designed and curated to complement the rest of the room.

Every aspect and element of decorating your tree is unique to your style. There is no right or wrong way. If your Christmas tree makes you happy when you walk into the room, it is exactly perfect.

A wee Christmas tree can be just as merry and festive as a larger one. The most fun part of a tiny tree is finding a unique container rather than the more common tree stand and skirt. Some choice looks can be fashioned with picnic baskets, tall baskets, old chippy buckets in all shapes and sizes, whiskey barrels, tureens, planters, crockery, and vintage wood crates. Look around to see what you can find and choose any container that speaks to your aesthetic.

A Mingle of Blues

A frosty flocked tree decorated with shimmering gold and white
ornaments creates a soft, snowy backdrop for a collection
of ribboned and beaded pale blue ornaments.
They mingle with a few collected blue mercury glass ornaments
for a pop of color and charm.

2 Vintage Toys

This tree is all about childhood Christmas magic. Inspired by
a set of old wooden toy ornaments my grandmother gave
me when I got married, this wee tree in the attic is covered
in little toy ornaments and retro baubles. The Santa topper also
belonged to Grandmother.

Classic Blue & White

A wonky-shaped natural tree is bejeweled with velvet ribbons
and a mix of solid blues and blue-and-white Delft.
The key is the layers of blue in the ribbons and ornaments,
from simple to embellished. My favorite part of this tree is the
antique chinoiserie planter that holds it; it was a housewarming
gift from my grandfather.

35

Romantic Floral Elegance

The look for this flower-filled Christmas tree in the greenhouse
started with a green tree that has an open shape, allowing for an
abundance of flowers to be tucked inside. An array
of stems of fresh hydrangeas, roses, and clusters of snowberry
and burgundy scabiosa are set in florist water vials. The tree is
held in an old cement basket planter.

Timeless Traditional

A favorite tree and a favorite look. The decorations are
collected vintage baubles and clear mini twinkling lights.
A lit pine cone garland on a lush, faux-fur rug adds a
layer of magic under the tree.

French Country Elegance

I love elegant Christmas as much as vintage.
Here layers of pearl-and-rhinestone garlands reflect the glow
of beautiful micro lights and tree candles, while gray velvet
ribbons add a touch of grace. A ruffled linen throw is a soft
skirt for cushioning pretty packages.

7 Natural Touches

A small, chubby tree is perfect for placing into an old wood crate for tabletop Christmas cheer. This tree is dotted with natural touches—wee pine cones, dried berry picks, and orange slices—mingling with small ornaments. Velvet ribbons in burnt orange and taupe and a couple of tiny vintage deer from my grandmother add the perfect finishing touches.

Ice Castle Aura

Sometimes simple decor is the perfect look for a Christmas tree. This snowy tree is decorated in shades of white and mercury glass ornaments, with faded dusty-blue velvet ribbons as the finishing touch. Setting the tree in front of a mirror adds another layer of magic through twinkle light reflection.

Kaleidoscopic Delight

Plenty of colorful vintage ornaments give this tree's imperfectly
perfect shape an abundance of Christmas cheer. Placed inside a
quaint bucket, it creates a delightful display in front of the
barn and is easy to tuck inside the doors if foul weather moves in.
A wood crate by the base of the tree is filled with ageless
baubles for another layer of charm.

10 Mushroom Enchantment

Covered in rich reds and navy blues, this tree is a favorite for
the moody backdrop of the cottage. Inspired by a set of
glass clip-on mushroom ornaments, I continued the nature-
inspired look with pine cones, berries, and branches. I layered
blue and black velvet ribbons for a bit of drama. Somewhat
unruly greenery on the mantel echoes the natural look.

Waterfall Shimmer

Decorated with vintage ornaments and draped in silvery tinsel,
this frosted tree shimmers and shines and brings a nostalgic
feeling to the dining room, where the cupboard is filled with a
wood house village that lights up for a magical display. Packages
are wrapped in pink butcher paper and tied with velvet.

12 Crimson Creation

Bold and beautiful, decorated with layers of rich reds and
whites for a tree full of Christmas merriment and joy.
Berry picks, vintage garlands, gingerbread house ornaments,
and little nutcrackers trim this tree. The secret to the swag
of red ornaments across the tree is four ornament garlands
tucked into the branches.

Silvery White Magic

The glow of a white Christmas tree absolutely lights up the
room. Set in a half whiskey barrel, the tree is dressed sparsely
with mercury glass ornaments, layered ribbons, and a few pieces
of shimmery tinsel. Layers of fringed rhinestone garland draped
on the branches finish the tree with a touch of elegance.

Angels of Light

Dainty ribbons and tree candles create a simple, more European
Christmas look. A set of vintage angel candleholders and angel
napkin rings from a thrift store became perfect ornaments on
this tree. I just added wire to loop them onto the branches
and brought in a few pearly stars for a lovely finishing touch.

Glimmers of Silver & Gold

Silver and gold are classic colors for Christmas trees, and this one was inspired by a basketful of star wind chimes found at a local tag sale. Originally, I had planned to remove the chimes and use just the metal stars as ornaments, but I liked the little extra oomph the chimes brought with their silver tone. When you walk by the tree, they glimmer along with the tinsel.

Moody Modern

Frosty blues and silvers are a pretty complement to a
snow-covered, flocked tree. With white berry and branches
picks, glittery detailed ribbons, and a wood bead garland,
this tree has a sophisticated look for those
who love rich colors like dark blues on a tree.

Verdant Glamour

A roll of olive-green velvet ribbon inspired this tree. Shades
of white, cream, and frosty metallic ornaments along with green
ribbon bows create a simply charming tree. On the mantel,
a mixed fresh eucalyptus garland is accented with long green
velvet ribbons to tie the look together.

Graceful Shades of Pink

The key to this look is using ornaments in various shades of the
same color and in assorted sizes and sheens to create a
pretty-as-a-picture tree. Ornaments in vintage pink mercury
glass, pearly white, and silver complement each other gorgeously.

19
Farmhouse Reminiscence

Red wood bead garland mixed with glass garland, along
with old and new red, white, and silver ornaments turn
out a traditional look by the barn. Simple gray ribbon
streamers add glamour.

20

Frosty Narrow

A frosty tree with a slender profile fits this little corner perfectly.
Next to an antique floral-painted armoire, the mingle of
classic blue ornaments and layered blue ribbons echoes the
details on the armoire for a charming look.

French Chic & Pearls

Dressed with glitz and a touch of French chic, this snowy
tree is well layered. Pearl garlands, mercury glass
ornaments, rhinestone snowflakes, and the palest blue
ribbons create an elegant look.

Imperfect Made Perfect

I have a soft spot for wispy trees, and this small tree by the
stairs is a favorite. I placed it inside an old picnic basket
for the base and dressed it with small silver and gold ornaments
and strings of gold glass garlands.

23

Collection Inspired

A collection of little antique putz houses, silver tinsel, and
rhinestone garland dress this spindly frosted tree. Set inside a
real tree-stump stand, it has a truly nostalgic look. The mirror is
draped in rhinestone and beaded garland, while the cupboard
has fresh greenery atop for even more Christmas cheer.

24

Fancy & Filled

Creating a mini forest in your home with more than one
tree is a luxurious, filled look. You can arrange two or more
trees in different sizes and decorate them the same,
or you could place another style tree in the backdrop of the
main tree for another layer of magic.

Wee Bucket Trees

Christmas cheer comes in all shapes and sizes, and smaller trees
bring a wealth of beauty to your home. Whether your main tree
is on the smaller side, or you are like me and want to
include Christmas all through the house, tabletop trees are
perfect for placing into interesting buckets, baskets, or crates for
a unique look anywhere in the house.

All through the House

While I go about chores or work from room to room, I like to enjoy the magic of Christmas all through the house.

That doesn't necessarily mean that each room has a tree or even a string of lights. It might be a sprig of pine tied to the sconces or a small wreath or bit of garland draped over a mirror. It is more about keeping that feeling of Christmas throughout the house so that, as you walk through, the feeling continues beyond the main living space.

One of my simpler ways to dress the house is to add fresh clippings, bowls of vintage baubles, and holiday flowers throughout. While some spaces get a bigger sprinkle of Christmas magic than others, I feel that each room deserves a little something.

OPPOSITE & OVERLEAF: A welcoming front door, whether it is done up with a wreath and garland or a small fresh tree standing sentinel, prepares guests for what they will experience inside your home.

Entry

OPPOSITE: Just through the entry, the inside door
frame is draped with a fresh garland and tied
with bows. A chunky basket holds a welcoming
Christmas tree done in a rustic elegant style.
Its branches are filled with natural touches, like
pine cones, dried hydrangeas, and dried berries.
The elegance comes from brassy, glittery gold
along with white ornaments and the cheery
greeting of a brass Merry Christmas sign tucked
in. Green satin ribbons and glass bird ornaments
echo the rustic-elegant natural look, and the tree is
topped with a glittering wire star.

THIS PAGE: On the table, I favor a bowl of
mercury glass ornaments or a vintage statue
wearing a fresh cedar crown. An antique gathering
basket on the wall is filled with fresh-clipped
seasonal greens and dotted with a few ornaments.

Hallway & Stairs

ABOVE AND OPPOSITE: I love traditional French-inspired Christmas decor on
the little staircase leading to the attic. This staircase doesn't get daily use during
the season, so, for a magical touch for a dinner party or Christmas Eve,
I love to add several battery candles on the treads. Of course, use caution
and stay with realistic-looking faux for safety anywhere you are enjoying candles.
For this special-occasion wedding gathering, I also placed several bouquets of
fresh flowers on the steps for a romantic look.

When it comes to garland on the staircase, think outside the box of traditional
Christmas greens. Beautiful garlands made with fresh flowers, baby's breath,
and eucalyptus bring a fresh and unique look.

OPPOSITE: Ribbons are one of my go-to elements for adding
that dash of glamour that is elemental to French Country
style. On the staircase garland, the ribbon has a loose drape
and a couple of colors are layered together for more glam.
The long ties provide a bit of drama.

ABOVE: On the vintage-inspired clock in the hallway, just a little sprig
of juniper tied with a ribbon is a simple touch of Christmas cheer.

Living Room

OPPOSITE AND ABOVE: I tend to decorate trees with the colors and feeling that
make them fit the everyday look of the room instead of packing things away
to allow for Christmas. The living room is full of bustle during the holiday season, and
the main Christmas tree takes center stage. A tree covered in beautiful fairy lights is
usually on repeat here, and placed in front of the stacked mirrors, its glow is echoed.
The twinkle enchantment seems to fill the room floor to ceiling.

The living room tree is our main, largest tree and is almost always decorated with
mercury glass ornaments in shades of white, silver, gold, and blush. I love an elegant
look and feeling for this room, so I like to include pearl and rhinestone garlands,
feathery beaded picks, and ribbons. Underneath, a ruffled linen throw is repurposed as
a skirt and covered with white and silver packages.

OPPOSITE & ABOVE: The fireplace dressed for Christmas looks
different each year. Sometimes it has a full garland that drapes;
other years it is more quietly dressed with a few sprigs of greenery.
I generally keep the fireplace decor simple with just candles, flowers,
and ornaments, with ribbons at the ends.

If using garland in front of a working fireplace where fresh dries
quickly, you can use a realistic faux garland and save the fresh
garlands for areas away from heat. Spritzing with water daily
will help keep a fresh garland longer. A tip is to keep garland on a
fireplace unadorned to allow for a quick and easy change when it
starts to dry. When using faux foliage, I like to add sprigs of fresh
greens to accent it and will often layer a fresh garland atop faux,
which makes it easy to remove and replace as needed.

Step-by-Step Tree Layering

Whether your usual Christmas tree is full and over the top or on the smaller side, decorating it is personal to each person or family.

The process of decorating a tree is about layering. You can choose which layers speak to you and leave the others behind.

Here are some tips:

* THE TREE: Which style tree to decorate is the first question. Do you want a flocked tree that looks like it has a layer of fresh-fallen snow or a traditional evergreen? There are spindly trees waiting to be loved to life and chubby trees with abundant branches. Once you decide and get it set up, the next step is the lights.

* LIGHTS: If you have a pre-lit faux tree, this step is done. If not, string your lights on the branches in a zigzag fashion, working from the inside toward the outer middle of the branches. Tuck the lights inside the tree rather than on the outer tips and take time to hide the wires. Use all one type of lights or mix and mingle.

* GARLAND: If you are using a garland with icicles or ornaments, this is a good time to add that layer so you don't have to move other decorations out of the way to place the garland later.

* ORNAMENTS: Think about placing ornaments in layers. Larger ornaments are best tucked into the lower branches and set inside the tree. Regular-size ornaments can go anywhere and can be grouped. Small or mini ornaments display well at the top of the tree and all over in groupings. I add them as a detail layer with the larger ornaments and usually a little further out on the branches so they can dangle. If you like icicles or drop ornaments, place those in areas where they will drape nicely, often toward the outer tips of the branches.

* CANDLES: Clip-on candles are a lovely touch of old-fashioned charm. Clip them all over for a beautiful glow.

* RIBBONS: These are one of my go-to finishers. Some are long and flowing; others are short and sweet. Tie them to the branches or pre-make the ribbons and use a hook to add them.

* TINSEL: For a vintage look, add tinsel after all the other decorations are on. Simply drape pieces where you would like a little extra movement.

* TREE TOPPER: If using a topper, you can add it first or last. I tend to add the topper last because I don't always use one and I like to see how the tree comes together before deciding.

* UNDER THE TREE: Whether to choose a skirt, a basket, a crate, an urn, or something else, choose what speaks to your overall look. A lighted garland underneath the tree adds a mesmerizing layer for nighttime.

Dining Room

ABOVE AND OPPOSITE: The dining room is always changing during the holidays. Depending on my mood, I might fill the 14-foot-long antique cupboard with unassuming white ironstone. Or I bring out some of the antique transferware I have collected to give the space a country look. I almost always clip fresh cedar from the yard to set on the shelves and often scatter fruit, anise pods, and nuts among the greenery or in bowls. Other times, just a few ornaments and greens will do.

ABOVE AND OPPOSITE: For these looks, lacy plates, gold
glasses, and antique crystal bring a festive Christmas feeling.

Kitchen

ABOVE AND OPPOSITE: The kitchen is where friends and family gather, where plates of cookies and treats are made. Some years, I have added a small tree in a crate on the nine-foot-long island or tucked it into a corner of the counter. Other years, just a holiday wreath or swag tied with a ribbon, a Christmas floral arrangement, and a bowl full of baubles seems just right.

ABOVE AND OPPOSITE: The easiest way to bring
a touch of the season in without overwhelming
your space is in small, quintessential bits: greenery
on the shelf, a copper colander or wooden bowl
filled with ornaments, a floral arrangement
you create yourself.

Bedroom

ABOVE AND OPPOSITE: The bedroom is one of my favorite places to add another tree and more Christmas charm. There is something about the glow of Christmas lights filling the room while you read in bed. And if you have a seating area with a working or faux fireplace, draping a garland and adding some stockings creates a perfect Christmas spot to enjoy all season long.

Garland for the Mantel

ABOVE AND OPPOSITE: Fresh garland on the mantel is always
a beautiful touch. This garland is a special order from the
flower market, a mix of different varieties of sage-color eucalyptus
and acacia. I love their soft color.

After draping the garland on the mantel, add long ribbons to each
end and tie them in loose bows. Tuck flowers into the garland,
using florist water vials for fresh blooms. Wire flowers in place,
and add candles for ambiance.

Office

Down the hall to the back bedrooms, I walk right past the office
on the way. So it always gets a little Christmas cheer.
A wispy Charlie Brown tree is a favorite look. Wearing vintage
ornaments and draped in beaded garlands and tinsel, it sits inside a
fanciful carved stand for a unique look. The antique cupboard
behind it gets a few baubles, fresh greenery, and ribbons.

Bathroom

ABOVE AND OPPOSITE: In bathrooms, simplicity
is key to keeping them feeling clutter free. A sprig
of fresh-cut pine tied with a ribbon for the mirror,
a fresh floral arrangement for the vanity, or a few
clippings or garland draped over the top of the mirror
are understated ways to welcome the season.

Attic

Our attic space has low ceilings and slanted walls; the cozy feeling always inspires me. Some years, our grown-up kids have stayed up in the attic bedroom while home for Christmas, so I always love to place a small twinkling tree upstairs to create a cozy Christmas hideaway.

For a bit of whimsy, my childhood dollhouse gets a sprinkle of Christmas cheer too. Small battery-operated fairy lights placed inside are set on a timer to create a nighttime glow, while a bottlebrush tree, Santa, and some presents are usually bedecking the porch.

Christmas in the Cottage

The guest cottage is a small house that was built in 1940, like our main home. It has wood plank walls and ceilings, exposed beams, and original elements mingling with vintage in the kitchen. The saturated color palette gives the cottage a slightly moody feel: charcoal bookcases in the living room and an original faded yellow cupboard in the kitchen inspire more color use in everyday and holiday decor.

The cottage door has a small pergola built around it, which provides some shelter from the weather and a place for the jasmine and roses to climb during summer. For Christmas, a drape of fresh, mixed garland is an unpretentious way to dress it up. The door wreath is enhanced with sugared fruit and is tied with a burnt umber velvet ribbon. Cast-iron candle lanterns simply tied with a sprig of greenery create a warm welcome.

In the living room, with the dark backdrop of the bookcases,
the tree takes on a moody look as well. It is covered in willow
branches, clusters of dried berries, and pine cone garland tucked
among the tree branches for a full look. Bright reds and glass
mushrooms add a bit of cheerfulness, and the navy and black
velvet ribbons are doubled for a little drama.

In the kitchen, sprigs of fresh greens tied with pine cones and an
ornament add a sweet touch on the cutting boards. Sometimes the
kitchen is dressed with a wreath in the window above the vintage
cast-iron sink; other times a fresh seasonal arrangement, fruit, and
a bowl of ornaments bring the merry and bright touch.

ABOVE LEFT: An unadorned wreath on the bathroom wall is simple and sweet. On a side table, a small bouquet and baubles are a little touch of Christmas.

ABOVE RIGHT AND OPPOSITE: In the bedroom, a simple arrangement of white and pink roses are on the nightstand, and layers of cozy blankets and French linens on the bed set a warm, comfortable mood.

OPPOSITE & ABOVE: Dried natural touches of the pampas grass and
faded eucalyptus garland inspired the bedroom tree. Decorations include
blush, gold, and cream ornaments along with vintage sugared fruit,
ribbons, and natural wood snowflakes. The faded color palette continues
under the tree, where the presents are wrapped in 1970 newspaper padding
from a box of wine glasses we bought.

French

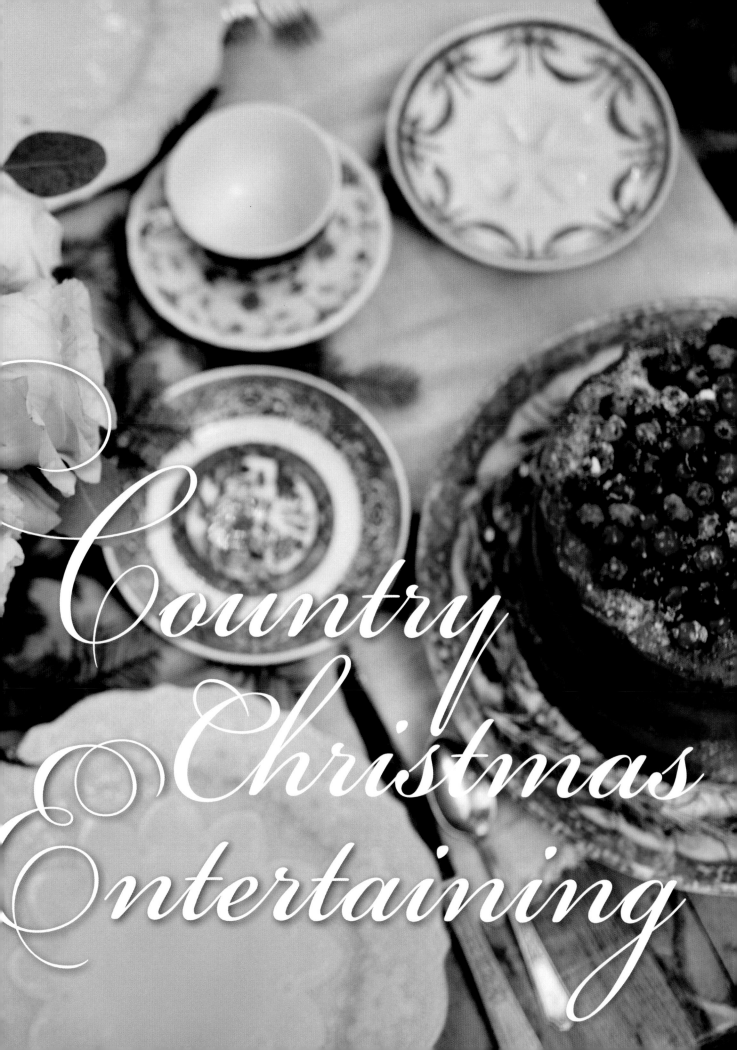

Country
Christmas
Entertaining

When planning for guests at Christmastime, first on my list is creating a beautiful ambiance—that means twinkling trees in the background, lots of candles or lights, and details like ornaments and fairy lights on the table. I hope the setting will inspire guests to linger longer, continue in conversation long past dessert while the candles burn low, and eventually depart feeling indulged and filled with beautiful memories.

Christmas place settings are where you can give way to your fancier-than-everyday side. Bring the gilded stemware and use all the extra layers for the place settings. Perhaps wrap napkins with a velvet ribbon. Or crown the place setting with a small detail like a millinery flower, a little wreath, or another decoration that can become a sweet takeaway for guests to enjoy at home.

Whether setting a table in a traditional dining space or outdoors, where weather allows, your Christmas table is about using what you love and creating a look that speaks to you.

Setting the Table

A few table setting tips:

✳ Indoors, think outside the dining room and set up a table in a different area for a fresh view.

✳ A garland on the table—fresh or faux—makes a simple centerpiece. Customize it with flowers, berries, or ornaments to create a look that fits your whole house decorating theme.

✳ Incorporate something unique into each place setting—an heirloom ornament, flowers, a sprig of greens, for example.

✳ Fresh-clipped greens tucked under the edge of each plate act as a "place mat" wreath.

✳ Tablecloths are optional. Use elegant linens or leave the table bare for a more casual feeling.

✳ Lighting equals warmth. Add candles or string lights to the table and backdrop lighting, such as a Christmas tree or fireplace, for coziness.

✳ Set up a bar cart and sideboard or side table for serving so your tabletop isn't too crowded for guests' comfort.

✳ It is all about the mix and mingle of decor. Don't be afraid to use nontraditional colors, to mix elegant pieces with rustic ones, or to combine new with vintage in your place settings.

✳ Music adds a sensory layer. Create several-hours-long playlists of holiday music to play in the background.

✳ If you don't have space for a large tree in your dining space, small trees can bring just as much charm.

✳ Decorate cupboards, chandeliers, and mirrors with fresh greens.

✳ When setting a table outdoors, choose a location that allows for comfort. For instance, a table near a firepit would provide warmth, and a basket full of throws would be thoughtful if there is a chill.

✳ If you don't have a power source nearby, use battery-powered lighting or bring a mini power station for plug-in elements like the Christmas tree.

✳ Have fun! The holidays are about enjoying time with family and friends, and the biggest gift of the season is being present in the moment.

Blue & White Table

Layers of vintage blue and white is a somewhat unexpected
look for Christmas that encourages using what you love for your
tables all year long.

Clippings of fresh greenery running down the table mingle
with an arrangement of white hydrangeas, roses, and greens,
along with a few sprigs of juniper with berries.

Romantic Country Table

Inspired by pastoral charm, this French country table setting is
all about rustic luxe and a touch of romance. Delicately
detailed plates, gilded wine stems, and flatware tied with satin
ribbon are offset with country linen napkins and pewter plates
for a French country feel.

Eucalyptus Garland Table

Not all holiday tables need traditional greens to feel festive.
This table by the barn has fresh eucalyptus garland with white
roses and candles as a centerpiece. Antique chairs brought
outside provide a comfortable place to sit, while a tree by the
barn and overhead lighting give warmth and festive cheer.

Gilded glasses and detailed linen napkins add an elegant, festive
touch to holiday place settings. Fresh eucalyptus garland
with roses and candles creates a simple centerpiece for an
outdoor Christmas gathering.

Blush Table

On our farmhouse table covered with a blush ruffled linen tablecloth, a large hydrangea floral arrangement of mixed Christmas greens and accents of burgundy berries takes the spotlight. The place settings are simple yet detailed, with intricately patterned plates layered with collected pieces of silver flatware.

OVERLEAF: A chocolate naked cake topped with sugared cranberries and sprigs of rosemary adds a luscious bit of beauty.

Rock Fireplace Table

Vintage green goblets, fresh greenery, and a pine cone garland
used on repeat create a fully layered table by the rock fireplace.
The glossy place settings are topped with a simple wood
cutout greeting. Mixed flatware and evergreen linen napkins
mingle with the goblets. A nature-inspired tree dotted with
hydrangeas, along with the crackling fire, make
a unique Christmas setting.

OPPOSITE: Vintage Franciscan green glass goblets are beautiful
for a Christmas table.

ABOVE: A stacked layer cake is festive with herb greenery
and pine cones. On top, sugar sprinkles and rosemary "trees"
create a snowy scene for a vintage Christmas deer that
was my grandmother's.

Brunch by the Fireplace

Boards of fresh fruit and bakery delights are perfect for more
simple gatherings. This brunch table is charmingly decorated
with juniper clippings and miniature gingerbread houses.

Special Occasion Table

For a formal look for Christmas, this table brings
stemware and four layers of elegance together
on a wood tabletop.

Glass plates embellished with platinum etching layer
beautifully with dainty detailed plates.

Kitchen Grazing Brunch

Fresh-baked everything that makes Christmas Day breakfast or brunch easy
was the inspiration for this setting. A layer of parchment or butcher paper rolled out
onto the island creates a place for layering all kinds of pastries and fresh baked goods.
Stacks of small plates, coffee cups, and fresh French pressed coffee at one end of the
of table allow guests to serve themselves.

161

The patina on this centuries-old farmhouse table
inspired me to leave the top bare and use that beautiful
wood as the backdrop for the place settings. A rustic
layer cake decorated with sugar roses and fresh roses
adds a touch of romance.

Layered fresh greenery dotted with mercury glass ornaments,
a few candles, and overhead lights make the ambiance.

Gold & Candles Table

With a centerpiece of a fresh cedar garland and candles in varying sizes and heights, this large table setting creates a beautiful glow. Regarding candles, a variety of containers and styles, from glass jars to tapers, creates interest. And safety first: never leave candles unattended or burn them in unsafe weather. Faux flickering candles will provide a similar effect.

Merry & Bright Table

With antique green transferware in the cupboard and fresh greens
on the table, this is all about traditional colors. Fresh Christmas
greens are dotted with citrus and star anise, while elegant place
settings include collected, vintage etched glasses for a sweet touch.

Candied-Nut Sweet Potatoes

4 whole sweet potatoes

1 cup walnuts, chopped

1/2 cup agave nectar or maple syrup

Cinnamon for sprinkling, optional

Cayenne pepper for sprinkling, optional

Preheat the oven to 350° F. Clean sweet potatoes and slice lengthwise in half. Place in a baking dish, cover, and bake for 30-40 minutes, until a fork inserts easily.

Meanwhile, mix the walnuts and agave together in a small bowl.

Remove sweet potatoes from oven and top with the nut mixture. Bake again, uncovered, for about 15 minutes.

Remove from oven and sprinkle lightly with cinnamon and/or cayenne pepper, if desired. Serve warm.

Grammy's Mashed Potato Casserole

5 pounds organic russet potatoes

8 ounces cream cheese

1 cup sour cream

2 tablespoons garlic salt, or more to taste

3–4 pats butter

Paprika for sprinkling, optional

Pepper, optional

Peel the potatoes, cut into chunks, and boil until tender. Drain and place into a mixing bowl and use an electric mixer to blend and mash.

Add the cream cheese and sour cream a little at a time and continue blending until potatoes are creamy. Add garlic salt and blend again.

Butter a 9 x 13 baking dish and spoon in the potatoes. Dot with a few small pats of butter on top and then sprinkle with paprika and pepper, if desired.

If baking right away, bake at 400° F for about 30 minutes, or until the top is browned. If baking later, cover and refrigerate; then bake at 400° for 1 hour, or until heated through and crusty on top.

Handmade

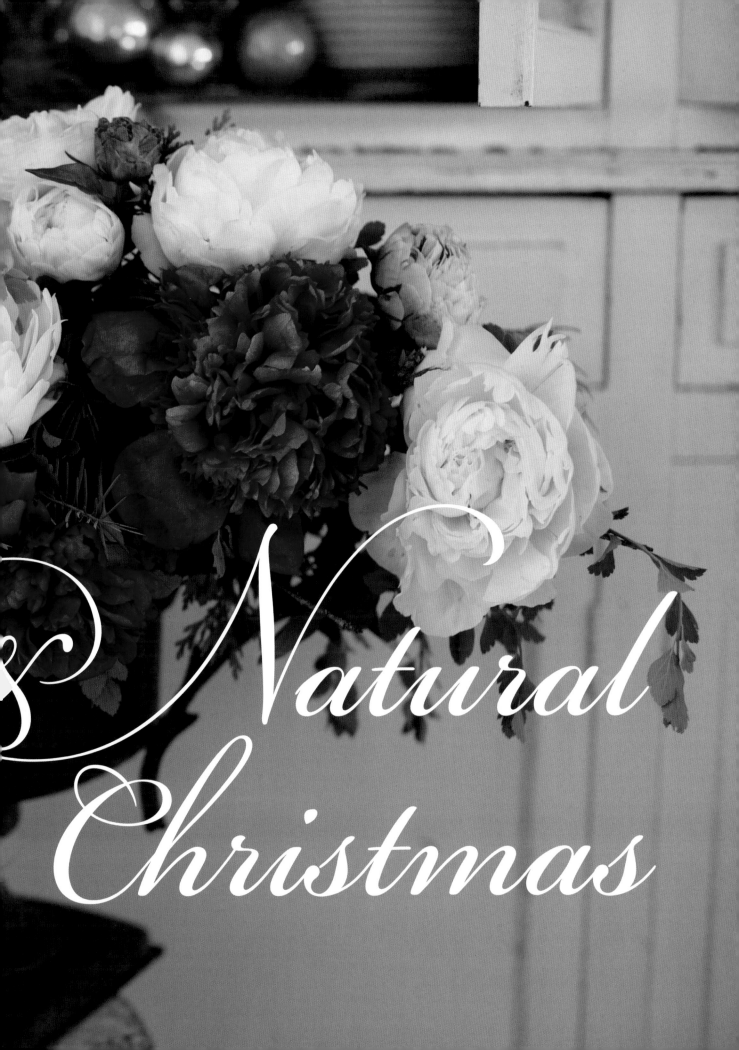

Natural
Christmas

*A*ll through the house is my motto for Christmas decor. I love that each time you walk through a doorway dressed in garland, pass a mirror with a fresh wreath, or walk toward a twinkling tree at the end of the hallway it really keeps the ambiance of Christmas around every corner.

My favorite small touches almost always involve fresh greens and other things nature supplies: small branches hung on the wall, containers filled with greens, or garlands decking the inside doors and windows; citrus, nuts, and pine cones along with ribbons but not much else for a simple, elegant look.

Here are a few ideas:

❋ Place greens at the top of a mirror; both garland and simple clippings work well. Add beads and baubles, velvet ribbons, or pine cones or leave unadorned for a natural look.

❋ Add a chunky branch or drape a garland across an interior doorway or window.

❋ Fill a wall basket with fresh or faux greens and add a few tiny ornaments for a festive touch.

❋ Tuck faux cedar branches into chandelier bases (make sure to keep away from light bulbs for safety).

❋ Place a wreath on a mirror or cupboard door.

❋ Lay fresh-clipped branches on shelves and add fresh fruit like oranges and pears; then sprinkle with whole nuts and pine cones.

❋ A basket of pine cones or fresh greens brings scent and charm.

❋ Pot several small trees of various sizes and group them together to create a winter wonderland.

❋ Gather bottlebrush trees to display with vintage putz houses in a cupboard or on a shelf.

Paperwhite Narcissus

ABOVE AND OPPOSITE: Paperwhites are some of my favorite flowers for the holidays. There is something so charming about their tall stems and dainty flowers.

To force the blooms for December, simply plant bulbs 4 to 6 weeks before you would like to enjoy them. They will grow in water, gravel with water, or soil. They are lovely planted in unique containers like teacups or transferware bowls.

Step-by-Step Table Centerpiece Garland

What you need:

Fresh or faux garland

Florist tubes for water if using fresh flowers

Orange slices, berries, fresh or faux flowers

A simple way to dress up a fresh or faux garland and make it all your own is to add flowers, citrus slices, ribbons, etc.

Start by laying your garland down the center of the table. Tuck in a few leafy stems.

Trim fresh flowers and tuck the stem into a florist tube filled with water. Or use faux flowers for a no-fuss look.

Add orange slices, anise pods, berries, and anything else you would like. You can either hot glue them into place or simply scatter them along the garland for a more natural appeal.

Customizing Wreaths

Fresh wreaths are easy to customize with fresh flowers or berries and foraged
leaves, nuts, and more. Start by wandering your yard and seeing what inspires you;
then tuck bits into a pre-made fresh or faux wreath for a unique look.

ABOVE: I designed this wreath (left) made with fresh mixed eucalyptus
and berries. It became part of my collection of faux Christmas foliage and
flowers available at Balsam Hill (right).

Dried Citrus & Wreaths

Dried orange slices and whole oranges are beautiful for
enjoying during the holidays. I use them to
accent side tables and garlands and even for creating
beautiful custom wreaths. For directions on
making dried oranges, see page 184.

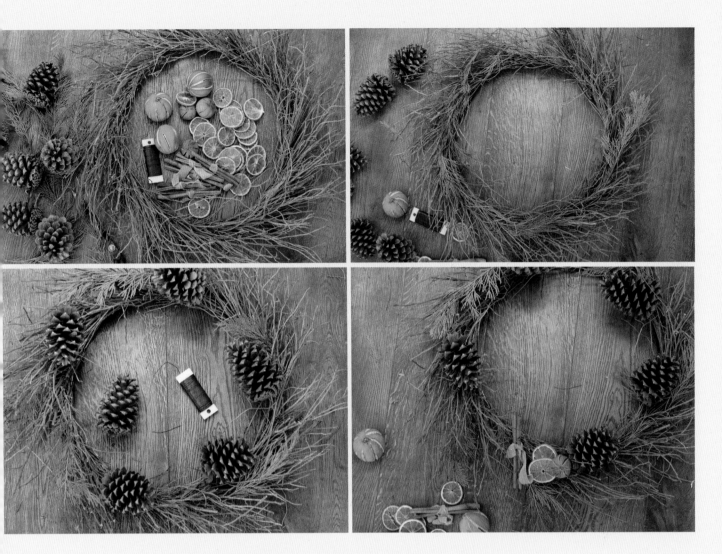

Step-by-Step Dried Citrus Wreath

Dried whole oranges and orange slices

Fresh-clipped Christmas greens, e.g., cedar or pine

Pine cones

Dried bay leaves

Velvet ribbon

Wire

Scissors

Hot glue gun and sticks

Start by adding the fresh greens to the vine wreath. Tuck in and then wire the pieces to the wreaths, or add with hot glue.

Next, loop a piece of wire around each pine cone, allowing enough wire to tie it firmly to the wreath. Repeat all around the wreath, filling in areas with pine cones.

Wire dried whole oranges to the wreath in the same way as the pine cones. The number of oranges is up to you, depending on the size of your wreath.

Hot glue the slices to the wreath, filling in the areas around the pine cones and whole oranges. Then hot glue dried bay leaves or similar, tucking them into the spaces between that need filling in.

Keep adding until you are happy with the look of the wreath. It can be decorated simply or fully, depending on what you prefer.

Tie a velvet ribbon bow and leave the ends long. Place it wherever you'd like and wire or hot glue it to the wreath.

Dried Whole Oranges and Slices

Oranges, whole

Oranges to slice

PREPARING ORANGES

For whole oranges, work evenly around each orange, making 4 cuts from top to bottom about 1/4 inch deep. Do not fully cut through the oranges. Then make 4 more cuts between the first ones, so there are 8 sections.

For thin slices, cut through the fruit crosswise, about 1/4 inch widths.

DRYING WHOLE ORANGES AND SLICES

Line a baking sheet with parchment paper.

Slice oranges thinly and lay them on the parchment paper in a single layer. Dehydrate in a 200° F oven for 3 to 4 hours, turning with a spatula every 30 to 45 minutes to prevent burning. Turn off the oven and let cool completely before removing.

FOR ORANGE POMANDERS WITH CLOVES

Using a zester or knife, slice any pattern or design you like on the peel of the fresh oranges. Insert whole cloves in the sliced areas and leave to air-dry or dry them in a food dehydrator. Set out in bowls or hang on the tree to scent your room.

Greenery with Fruits & More

ABOVE AND OPPOSITE: On the front porch, fresh cedar greens
and fruit are often on repeat for a simple, natural holiday display.
The planters are filled with greens and a few pine cones,
branches, and fresh oranges.

There are window boxes on nearly every window in the house.
For Christmas they are arrayed with fresh-clipped branches and
layered with pine cones, fresh fruits, and faux sugared fruits along
with hydrangeas. The window wreath is fresh eucalyptus and
mixed greens from the flower market.

Open Cupboards

ABOVE AND OPPOSITE: Inside cupboards and open shelves
are often overlooked for Christmas decorating. Whether using
antique dishes, copper, or another favorite collection, you can
create a charming vignette with clipped greens, fruits, and
whole nuts. Lay the greens down first and then arrange pears,
oranges, clementines, and whole nuts. Other natural
elements could be rose hips from the garden, whole artichokes,
dried berries and flowers, mossy branches, or anything else
that speaks to you.

Pretty Packages

Pretty papers, ribbons, and package toppers
create beautiful gifts. There are so many ways to
wrap packages; some of my favorites are
with simple, vintage-inspired prints, masking
papers, textured wallpapers, and, of course,
traditional colors and patterns. Collect bits
of ribbons and millinery flowers,
pins, ornaments, small pine cones, and other
natural bits throughout the year and set aside for
using on packages during the holidays.

Salt Dough Ornaments

2 cups flour

1 cup salt

1 cup water

Cookie molds or cutters

Paint and sealant spray, if desired

String or ribbon

Creating unique ornaments is a fun way to dress up packages or place settings or for gifting to friends and family. This craft is ideal for all ages, and salt dough is easy to customize with colors and scents, if you would like.

Mix the flour and salt together in a bowl. Slowly add 1 cup water, mixing as you go to make sure you don't use too much. Knead the mixture until it forms a dough.

Roll the dough onto a flat surface and use cookie cutters or detailed cookie molds to make your ornaments.

Using a straw, make a hole at the top of the ornament. Bake in a 250° F oven for about 2 hours, or until dry (depending on the thickness of your ornaments).

Let cool before decorating or painting. Spraying with a craft sealant will help them last. Add a ribbon for hanging on the tree.

Christmas

Cheer
Outdoors

The week before Christmas is full of traditions and childhood memories for me—baking cookies, watching favorite holiday movies, and soaking up the anticipation of the big day being just a few sleeps away. One of my favorite activities when I was little was hopping into the car to drive through the neighborhoods and look at the lights, bundled up in our Christmas jammies, with hot cocoa in hand and Christmas music playing on the radio. My dad would slow the car to almost a stop when there was a showstopper house. Sometimes it was a yard full of magical Christmas displays and sometimes it was a house with string lights framing the roofline and every window, looking like a fairytale cottage.

We continued that tradition with our children, and even as adults now, driving through neighborhoods to enjoy all the festive displays of Christmas cheer is a fun thing to do.

Merry and bright decorations outdoors come in all shapes and sizes. Maybe you deck the halls outside with lights on gables, outdoor trees, and wreaths at every window in full *Christmas Vacation* style. Maybe it is a simpler look with fresh greenery on the front door. Or maybe it is somewhere in between. There is no right or wrong way to dress your home indoors or outdoors for the holiday season; it is truly about your personal style and what you enjoy.

The Barn

We love to dress the outbuildings on our property.
We joke that our silkie chickens and goats love the festive glow
from the barn that is next to them. Strands of lights trace the
roofline, and the porch gets a twinkling tree all its own.
Placing an outdoor tree on a rolling stand is a simple way to
enjoy a tree outdoors yet be able to easily tuck it inside if the
weather turns rainy or snowy.

ABOVE AND OPPOSITE: Inside the barn, the antique French
mirror in the background is draped in fresh cedar garland
with layers of gold glass, beaded, and lit garlands for
a whimsical backdrop. An antique drapery
table is set for a festive gathering. Star lights woven through
the garland make it a magical centerpiece.

The Potting Shed

Our cedar shake potting shed gets a little bit of Christmas spirit,
from decorating the front porch with a large tree potted inside
a half whiskey barrel to a small tree inside a vintage cart.
This little shingled building is near the greenhouse and is where
we store all the garden tools for the winter season. It's also a
favorite little spot to decorate all year long.

ABOVE Enjoying a moment with Frizz on the
potting shed porch.

OPPOSITE: The small tree in a vintage cart can be moved
around to any location that suits my fancy!

The Greenhouse

Our greenhouse is often full of pots and plants that are growing or being stored over the colder season. But during the holidays, it also gets a little sprinkle of Christmas enchantment. Inside, a tree is set in a vintage cement basket pot and decorated with layers of fresh flowers and greens. Hydrangeas, snowberries, scabiosa, and roses are tucked into the branches to create a "blooming" Christmas tree. Florist water vials keep the flowers fresh longer, though the hydrangeas will dry beautifully without any water. The finishing touch of rich green velvet ribbons adds to the stately tree.

OPPOSITE: Outside the greenhouse, a frosted tree is decorated with soft, natural colors for a little bit of festiveness in the garden.

Snowberries are ideal for tucking into Christmas arrangements
and into the tree, where they add an exquisite natural touch.

Away
for

While the halls are decked at home for Christmas, many families load up their car and travel to visit family. Simple and sweet decor for a travel trailer is a happy way to enjoy the holidays while on the road. A camping spot by a mountain lake becomes a magical woodland Christmas with a twinkling tree and string lights draped along the trailer. After snowy weather wraps up, the glow from the cabins across the lake and a tree placed on the dock creates a winter wonderland scene.

Back home in California, a 1940s cabin in the woods of Lake Tahoe, covered in fresh snow, creates an idyllic Christmas scene. Original wood floors and planked walls are a beautiful backdrop for festive holiday decor. With antique and collected furniture filling the rooms, salvaged architectural elements, and a snowy landscape outside, this is a cozy place to enjoy the holidays.

Ultimately, anytime of year, my heart yearns for Paris. Tucked inside a charming apartment just steps from the Eiffel Tower, we decked the halls for a beautiful holiday. In keeping with the beauty and inspiration that Paris offers, the Christmas trees were decorated simply with natural touches, and it was all about fresh foliage and fruits that set the table for a patisserie-filled brunch.

Christmas on the Road

ABOVE & OVERLEAF: A 1960s shiny silver Avion travel trailer becomes almost like a parade float wearing its Christmas dress. With a strand of twinkle lights and a dazzling tree, this little camping spot by the lake feels full of holiday joy. The picnic table is set for a meal with friends and family. A fresh garland with candles creates a simple centerpiece, and the pewter place settings bring a silvery charm. Tartan throws are perfect for sitting on and wrapping in by the campfire as the evening chill sets in.

OPPOSITE: As if on cue . . .

Christmas at the Cabin

ABOVE: This rustic cabin's original and natural touches
are a homey backdrop for holiday decor.

OPPOSITE: A snowy tree on the porch welcomes guests
as they arrive.

ABOVE: The wood stove is cozy and nostalgic in every way, and boughs of greenery bring scent.

OPPOSITE: A small potted tree wearing red and white ornaments and a fresh garland on the shelf bring Christmas cheer to the bedroom.

OPPOSITE AND ABOVE: On the antique hutch, layers of
fresh greens and mercury glass ornaments in bowls create a festive
backdrop for the table. A wispy tree set inside a vintage picnic
basket is simply decorated with old-timey green ornaments.

ABOVE LEFT: A wee deer and tiny baubles create a charming moment on the shelf.

ABOVE RIGHT: Candle lights and a bit of greenery festoon the chandelier.

LEFT: The table in the kitchen is set for brunch with a deep green cloth and layers of vintage elements.

OPPOSITE: A sweet little A-frame outbuilding announces Christmas in a big way.

Christmas in Paris

ABOVE: When the sun sets and the Eiffel Tower lights up, the dining area
is perfect for enjoying the tree against the backdrop of Paris magic.

OPPOSITE: A tree dressed with fresh flowers and ribbons fills the corner
of the dining room, creating a beautiful look for entertaining.

OPPOSITE: The living room tree was decorated simply with paper honeycomb ornaments, dried orange slices, and velvet ribbon bows. A dotting of candles provided a glow for extra ambiance.

ABOVE: Fresh flowers are a must for me in decor, even during the holidays. This arrangement was created with fresh eucalyptus, wax flowers, and white roses picked up at a local florist.

Melty Camembert

Wheel of Camembert cheese

Honey

Fresh herbs

Salt and pepper

Fresh bread, sliced

Preheat oven to 350° F. Remove plastic covering from cheese and arrange back into its wooden box, lining with baking paper or foil if desired. Score or slice rind off the top. Leave cheese as is, or drizzle with honey and sprinkle with fresh herbs, pepper, jam, or any other toppings you desire. Bake for about 15 minutes, being careful not to overbake, or it will become more solid. Serve with fresh crusty bread and fruit.

OPPOSITE: This bistro table on the balcony is perfect for enjoying a simple plate of fruit and melted Camembert cheese with fresh bread.

PREVIOUS OVERLEAF, OPPOSITE & ABOVE, & OVERLEAF:
In the kitchen, a zinc-covered farm table is set for breakfast. A
centerpiece garland of fresh eucalyptus is dotted with pears and
roses from the market, while fresh bakery delights and French
press coffee are on repeat to start the day.

The scene from our balcony was a beyond lovely.
Of course, the pièce de résistance in the City of Light
is the incredibly beautiful architecture.

Resources

Links and details for specific items can be found at www.frenchcountrycottage.net in Resources.

Below are the places I regularly utilize for all types of decor items:

AMAZON—rhinestone garlands, velvet ribbons, holiday decor, dough molds

ANTHROPOLOGIE—primrose mirror, ornaments

ARTE ITALICA AND CROWN LINEN—gold, platinum, and lace-detail place setting elements, napkins, linens, and velvet stockings

AVE HOME—tall blue and gold reproduction mirror

BALSAM HILL—artificial Christmas trees, new ornaments, wreaths and garlands, lit houses, bottlebrush trees, stockings, skirts, and other holiday decor

THE BELLA COTTAGE—vintage and vintage-inspired decor and furniture

CRATE & BARREL—large, chunky-knit stockings

eBAY—vintage ornaments, vintage architectural elements

ELOQUENCE- European antique and reproduction furniture and decor

ETSY—vintage ornaments and vintage Christmas

FRENCH COUNTRY COTTAGE—custom linens, floral and matelassé stockings, ruffled linen chair slipcovers and tablecloths

FRENCH COUNTRY COTTAGE AT BALSAM HILL—eucalyptus and berry wreath and foliage

THE GRAND COLLECTIVE—various vintage decor and elements

THE HOME DEPOT—various home and holiday decor and fresh foliage

HOMEGOODS—holiday decor, antique-style mirrors, everyday decor items

PACIFIC COAST EVERGREEN—fresh wreaths, garlands, and foliage

PARIS RESOURCES- local shops, Balsam Hill France, Paris Perfect

SAN FRANCISCO FLOWER MART—fresh flowers

SUMMER COTTAGE ANTIQUES—vintage decor and elements

TARGET—holiday and home decor, artwork

THRIFT STORES AND TAG SALES—vintage ornaments, vintage decor elements, vintage linens, etc.

Acknowledgments

Thank you to my family. You are my biggest inspiration every day.

To Raymond, thank you for always supporting me and helping make all my crazy ideas and magical Christmas scenes come to life. I could not have put this book together without all your help.

To my children and your families—Ryan and Katt, Cullan and Diem, Ansley and Harley—thank you for embracing family dinners by Christmas-tree light all year long and, of course, for our littlest loves, Juliette, Enzo, and Jionni, who bring so much joy.

To my parents and siblings, thank you for inspiring me from youth to believe in the magic of Christmas and encouraging me to follow my dreams.

To Jill Cohen, thank you for helping to make another book a reality.

To Madge Baird for your support and patience with me and my creative process, to Rita Sowins for a lovely book design, and to all the folks at Gibbs Smith who helped this book come together.

To my Balsam Hill family, thank you for sending Christmas trees across the pond for our photo shoot and for our projects all year long. I am grateful for your support of this book and of me, always.

To Paris Perfect Rentals, appreciation for the most beautiful apartment with a view for our Christmas location in Paris.

To Michelle and Scott McCauley, thank you for your friendship and letting us borrow your idyllic snowy cabin in the woods.

To Victoria and Arte Italica Crown Linen, thank you for the most beautiful place setting elements and linens for our tables.

To my French Country Cottage friends and community, my gratitude for your friendship. Thank you for taking time to read my blog, for your kind notes, and for supporting my books and French Country Cottage everywhere. French Country Cottage would not be what it is without you!

About the Author

Courtney founded the lifestyle blog and brand *French Country Cottage*—a place inspired by renovations of her 1940s cottage and living a lifestyle that is fueled by inspiration and the romance that comes with it. She loves the quintessential mix of rustic and elegant elements such as an opulent chandelier against weathered wood, indulges a love of all things sprinkled with ambiance, and believes that a chandelier and bouquets of fresh flowers belong in every room.

In addition to working as a blogger, she works freelance as a photographer and stylist. Her work has been featured in magazines, catalogs, and on websites in the United States and Europe. A mom of three grown children, Courtney lives on a little slice of the countryside in California with her husband. She loves to travel and discover new inspirations, and you can often find her, camera in hand, playing with flowers. Connect with Courtney on her blog, *frenchcountrycottage.net*, and on Facebook and Instagram at French Country Cottage.

First Edition

23 24 25 26 27   5 4 3 2

Published by
Gibbs Smith
P.O. Box 667
Layton, Utah 84041

1.800.835.4993 orders
www.gibbs-smith.com

Designed by Rita Sowins / Sowins Design
Printed and bound in China

Gibbs Smith books are printed on either recycled, 100% post-consumer waste,
FSC-certified papers or on paper produced from sustainable PEFC-certified
forest/controlled wood source. Learn more at www.pefc.org.

Library of Congress Control Number: 2023930173
ISBN: 978-1-4236-6257-0